Free Money to Buy You

(A Step-by-Step Guide)

by

LeTicia Lee

www.SoRichIam.com

Free Money to Buy Your Fir$t Home

(A Step-by-Step Guide)

Published by:

SoRichIam.com Media

P.O. Box 20711

Rochester, New York 14602

www.SoRichIam.com

ISBN-13: 978-1497395039

ISBN-10: 1497395038

© 2014 All Rights Reserved

DISCLAIMER: The information herein is intended for educational purposes only. Please refer to the specific grant requirements in your intended city of home purchase. You should seek a real estate attorney for advice before completing any home purchase.

In my Father's house are many mansions.

If it were not so, I would tell you. I go to prepare a place for you. John 14:2

Table of Contents

Chapter	Page
Who Qualifies?	9
Benefits	11
Get Free Credit Report	13
Home Buyer's Assistance	17
First Time Home Buyer's Club	21
Employer Assistance Initiative	25
Build Credit	29
Home Counselor Interview	33
Homeownership Workshop	37
Get Pre-Approved	41
Home Search	45
Purchase Offer	51
Grant/Mortgage Approval	57
Title Documents	61
Homeowner's Insurance	65
Closing	69
Move In!	71
Post Purchase Workshop	75
Closing Remarks	79
Check List	83

It's true. There is free money available to buy your first home!

That means you don't have to pay it back!

How to Use this Workbook

The purpose of this workbook is to help you prepare for the home purchase process. You may be tempted to just skip to getting the grant applications and search for a home. However, we are providing a checklist of the items you will likely be asked along the way. (***See Check List on page 83***) Our intent is to help expedite the process and help you succeed in receiving this free money should you decide the terms and long term benefits are for you.

Review the workbook. Apply to programs for which you qualify. Use the checklist. Stay organized. Be patient.

Many of you can shave off years of scratching and saving to buy your first home. This book will show you how. Select the program(s) that are right for you.

With a little due diligence, you can be a home owner within the next year or two for no more than what you are currently paying in rent. Stay focused. Don't give up.

Notes

Who qualifies for this FREE Money?

- Working Full Time or Part Time
- College and High School Graduates
- Newlyweds
- New Parents
- Single Parents
- Single People
- Retired
- Self-Employed/ Entrepreneur / Business Owner
- Recovering from Bankruptcy
- Social Security
- Pension
- SSI
- Disability
- Workmen's Compensation
- Alimony
- Child Support

See your local program(s) for specific guidelines.

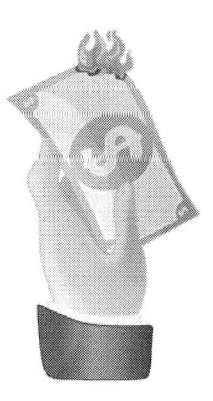

This is a great way for many people to get started or start over!

What you'll learn:

- ➢ Learn How you May Qualify for this Free Money.
- ➢ Learn Where to Find this Free Money.
- ➢ Learn How to Get this Free Money.
- ➢ Learn How to Get the Most Value with this Free Money.

Benefits

Own Faster:

Most people have to wait years just to come up with the down payment and closing costs of their first home purchase. In addition, many need additional funds for home renovation updates.

These programs will help cover most if not all of the down payment, closing costs, and home renovations. Have pride of ownership and build your home equity while you help build your local and national economy.

Home Improvement Grants:

Additional funds may be available to cover home improvements such as new roof, siding, windows, furnace and other energy savers. These programs are to help you improve the curb appeal of these homes. Occupied homes are happier homes.

Build Economy:

You'll be helping to build your local community and thus the national economy. This helps create jobs in the community (*home improvements etc.*).

More Value:

Many people find that they save more money as homeowners than they did paying rent. You get more value for your money and tax deductions (*interest and taxes*) too.

Build Retirement Savings – Invest - Save for College:

Eventually you will build equity in your home and increase your personal net worth. For many people, they find they are able to save more money towards retirement, invest more, as well as build college savings for their children.

If you're ready to own a home and it's your first home purchase, or if you have not personally owned a home in the last three years, herein are just a few steps to help you get started. Use this workbook to keep track of your progress.

You've already taken the first step. You've decided to be a homeowner.

<u>Notes</u>

Step 1 - Get a Copy of your Credit Report

You get one free copy of your credit report each year. Go online and contact all three simultaneously or contact each individually. (See **www.AnnualCreditReport.com**)

The three main credit reporting agencies are as follows:

- Equifax
- Experian
- TransUnion

Once you receive your credit report, make sure the information is accurate. If anything needs to be updated, including your current address, this is the time to do it.

Your credit report shows all outstanding debts, and whether or not you pay on time. If there is any inaccurate information, contact the company where the debt exists and get it corrected. You can also become more aware of your spending habits and see if there any areas that need improving or debts that need to be paid off.

Many students and newlyweds find that they have little or no credit. This is a good time to begin establishing credit, which will help reflect your level of responsibility of owning a home.

Don't worry if you have bad credit or no credit. You may still qualify. *(See Building Credit on Page 29)*

Note: **The Answer Key to Avoid Debt, Build Credit & Retire Rich** includes additional steps on how to build your personal credit. Find it at www.SoRichIam.com

Work Sheet

Include any creditors with whom you need to resolve issues.

Work Sheet

Step 2 – Home Buyer's Assistance

Local City Government:

Go to your local city government's website. Search for **Home Buyer's Assistance Programs.** Your local city government website may also include the requirements to participate in the program. While most of them are for low and moderate income people, couples, and families, there are some with no income limits too.

View what programs they offer and some of the renovated properties they offer to first time home buyers. You can purchase properties outside of this list also. Some may need renovation, but there is also *free money* available to do minor repairs which can be very helpful.

Request an Application:

Either download an application from the website or call the real estate/housing development department to request an application be mailed to you.

Local Non-Profit Organizations:

Your city should also be familiar with local non-profit organizations that also offer funding. Ask who they are and visit their websites also. Many of these grants can be used together. If you don't have a computer, call or visit to schedule an appointment.

Complete and Submit your Application:

Make a copy of your blank home buyer's assistance application(s). This is just in case you have any errors. Make sure your application is neat and legible.

Do not send original copies of any of the items they request of you. Keep a copy of the completed application for your records. Submit your application by mail or in person.

Follow up to make sure all required items have been received. Ask for an appointment with a Housing Counselor. Most will call you once your application has been reviewed to schedule your appointment.

Keep track of your application and appointments. Be on time.

Work Sheet

Do you qualify for any Home Buyer's Assistance Programs? If so, which ones?

_____
_____
_____
_____
_____
_____
_____
_____
_____
_____
_____
_____
_____
_____
_____
_____
_____
_____
_____
_____
_____
_____
_____
_____
_____
_____
_____
_____
_____

Work Sheet

Step 3 – Join a First Time Home Buyer's Club (Bank/Credit Union)

These are banks and credit unions that offer matching funds to potential first time home buyers as well as people who may not have owned a home in at least three years. Search for banks or credit unions in your area which offer **"First Time Home Buyer Clubs"**. Your city Home Buyer's Assistance Program may have a list of banks and credit unions in your area currently offering a first home buyer's club program. Just ask.

Matching Gifts:

Many banks and credit unions offering first time home buyer's clubs will match your funds up to four to one! That means for every dollar you deposit, they will add four dollars with a minimum monthly deposit required. This has made many renters home owners in a very short period of time.

It may take 10-24 months to complete the program, but it's to your advantage. There is a specified minimum you must deposit each month but you will see it again multiplied.

After you complete the first time home buyer's club program, you will find a property you desire to purchase. The bank will provide their matching funds to your account to help cover part or all of your down payment, closing costs, and in some cases, associated workshop fees. Whether you are single, married, starting a family or just starting over, this can be very helpful.

Set Up Auto-Deposits:

Your Payroll Department can help you set up automatic deposits into this account by deducting a portion from each paycheck. This way you will not miss any payments. Missed deposits may disqualify you from this program.

Many first time home buyer clubs will even have a trial period (approx. three months) to make sure you can handle the monthly commitment. If you decide not to complete the program for any reason, you still keep the money you saved. But if you spend any of it before the program is complete, especially if it's not used for the home purchase process, you may be disqualified.

They want to see that you can be responsible and make consistent payments on your mortgage later. After all, they will be adding funds to your account once you prove you are ready and serious about being a home owner.

Mortgage Lender:

Most first time home buyer clubs require you to apply for your mortgage with them as part of the criteria for acceptance. Shop around. Select the bank/credit union that offers the best terms and mortgage rates before applying to the first time home buyer's club.

Second Position Grant Lien:

Most first time home buyer clubs (banks/credit unions) require you to also live in the property for a minimum period of at least five years. See specific terms of participation. The minimum living terms are in fine print. Once you've lived in the property for the minimum agreed term to satisfy your free money grant, be sure this second lien is removed.

You will have to remember to do this yourself. This will prevent problems later should you decide to sell your home.

Continue saving money every month after you complete the program.

You'll be amazed at how much you save towards retirement!

Work Sheet

Compare first Time Home Buyers Clubs in your area. Choose one that works best for you.

Step 4 – Employer Assistance Initiative

Employer Assistance Initiative:

Some employers provide an **employer assistance first time home buyer's program**. There is usually no income limit to join this program.

They often work in conjunction with the city to match funds they offer towards your down payment and closing costs and sometimes more.

Stable employees make better employees. Working people help stabilize the housing market and build the local economy. Everyone benefits.

Human Resources Department

Go to your Human Resources Department to see if they offer an **employer assistance first time home buyer's program**. Sign up for any matching funds 401k programs if they offer that too. If so, get started! It's GREAT motivation to work for a company that has invested in your personal well-being.

Work Sheet

Does your employer offer matching funds to first time home buyers? Do they offer a matching funds 401k? If so, what do you need to get started?

_____
_____
_____
_____
_____
_____
_____
_____
_____
_____
_____
_____
_____
_____
_____
_____
_____
_____
_____
_____
_____
_____
_____
_____
_____
_____
_____

Work Sheet

Step 5 - Build Your Credit

Revolving Credit:

Many first time home buyers have not yet established their credit. This is a good time to do it.

You need to maintain at least three lines of credit. These are items you pay monthly and on time to sustain good credit. Most of these free money grants expect applicants to have a minimum credit score of 620 or higher.

If you have a monthly cellular phone bill, gas and electric bill, student loan payment, car loan, internet or cable bill, these are used to help establish your credit. However, the most popular "revolving lines of credit" are major credit cards, department store credit cards, and gas cards.

If you don't' have any of the above types of credit established yet, get a credit card from your local department store or family store such as Walmart, Sears, Kmart, Kohl's or Target. These family stores are useful later as you can purchase items for your new home. If you own a car, consider getting a gas card. It's something you already purchase. Don't max out these credit cards. Pay the bill every month on time and in full.

You only need one major credit card (Mastercard, Visa, American Express). You may have to start with a department store credit card before applying for a major credit card. If you are already paying high interest on your credit cards, and pay on time, see if you can get the interest rate lowered. If your credit card company won't lower the interest rate (below 10% for good credit or 11-19% for low or bad credit), see what others offer lower rates. Transfer your debt to a lower Annual Percentage Rate (APR) card if you can.

Make sure you have the lowest possible interest rates for which you qualify. See your bank. Many times, if you already have an account with your bank, they will offer you better rates to keep your business.

Establish Good Credit for Better Mortgage Rates Later:

The First time Home Buyers Club also helps build your credit. That looks good on your credit report. Many employers now also check our credit report to see if you are a responsible person. So you are building credit and setting yourself up for better job opportunities later too.

Points are deducted every time someone checks your credit. Wait a few months (3-6 months) before applying for a pre-approval mortgage for your home loan.

Work Sheet

How many credit cards do you have? List them here. Include your credit limit, interest rate, and how much you owe. Which ones have super high interest rates? Which ones can you eliminate? Can you get lower interest rates? Keep track of your expenses.

Work Sheet

Step 6 - Interview with Home Counselor

You've already reviewed the program qualifications and completed the application. Now, you'll meet with the Home Buyer's Assistance Counselor.

They want to make sure you understand the commitment you're making. They are helping you pay for your first home. They expect you to take care of it inside and out. That helps increase property values, decrease the housing debt, and build the local economy.

Don't think for one minute they are doing you a favor. You are helping the city clean up. Therefore, choose a property you really like so you can feel good about doing your part.

Be patient as they go down the obligatory checklist of items you must complete and the workshop(s) you must attend depending on your property purchase, and program(s) for which you qualify. All of this is to ensure your long term home purchase success.

Single - Double – Multi-Family Home

While most of you will be purchasing a single family residential home, some may be purchasing a double or multi-unit owner occupied home. That means you may have a single property with several units of which you occupy one. It's a great way to have tenants in another unit that pay part or all of your mortgage. If you are considering the purchase of a double or multi-unit home, you will likely need to attend an additional workshop for landlords.

Unfortunately, many of the neglected properties are owned by out of town owners who collect the rent and neglect the necessary property upkeep. That won't be you. The city wants to make sure that you have a vested interest in your property. Therefore, you must live on the premises. Hopefully, you will be more attentive to the upkeep.

Have a clear idea what type of property you will be pursuing before your interview so your housing counselor can select the appropriate workshop for you to attend. If you are even considering a double or multi-unit owner occupant home, say so. If this is the case, sign up for the home owner and landlord workshops. It saves time later while you're searching for a home.

Work Sheet

Get clear on what type of property you want and/or need. Decide if you prefer single residence or if you can handle being a landlord of a double or multi-unit property. Understand the commitment and responsibility of each. Learn what grants are available and what workshops you must attend to meet the criteria for each.

Step 7 – Attend Homeownership Workshop

Most of you will be attending a one or two day workshop to review the homeowner's program guidelines and the general home buying process. This is usually a full day workshop so plan accordingly.

Reimbursement for Workshop Fees:

Depending on where you live, there may or may not be a workshop fee. Some first time home buyer's clubs will reimburse you at the end of the program. Just save the receipt.

Ask the home buyer counselor when you schedule the class if there is an associated workshop fee. If so, tell your first time home buyer's club bank representative. They will tell you if the workshop fee can be paid by using your available saved funds.

Don't ask your friends. Each program has its own criteria. Ask your home owner representative or bank only.

Commitment, Pride and Responsibility:

The free money is for people who are willing to maintain these properties and in turn increase property values. General maintenance is a collective effort between the city or town you live in and the people who are willing to take responsibility for the general upkeep of these properties.

Have the pride of home ownership. Build equity. Build your credit.

Those who can handle the additional responsibility of being a good landlord may also enjoy having additional income. Some are even able to live free as the rent they collect from the other units covers all or part of the entire monthly mortgage payment.

Owning a home is often more affordable than renting. Homeowners also receive the benefits of having an annual tax write off. *(Speak to your accountant.)*

Work Sheet

Work Sheet

Step 8 – Get Pre-Approved for a Home Loan

Once you've completed your home buyer's assistance application and homeownership workshop, you'll be more clear on what grants you will be applying to your home purchase costs. If you're participating in the first time home buyer's club, you may want to wait until you are near your last month to get pre-approved for a home loan. You need to know the price range of properties you qualify to purchase.

Your credit report/score is only good for sixty days. So if it's been over two months since your bank pulled it to start your home buyer's club account, they will likely pull it again.

Credit Score 620 or better:

You don't want too many companies pulling your credit report as it lowers your score. If you've been building your credit and paying your bills on time, you should be okay. Most banks and home buyer's assistance programs require a credit score of at least 620.

Pre-Approval Mortgage Letter:

Based upon certain variables such as income, credit score, and the amount of time you've lived in your current location, they will give you an estimate of how much they may approve for your home loan. This is only a seventy five percent assurance as you will not receive final approval until you have selected a home to purchase and they have inspected the property. Meanwhile, get a copy of the Pre-Approval Home Mortgage Letter from the bank/credit union and keep a copy with you when you search for a home.

Realtors will want to know how much you are pre-approved for so they can show you properties within your price range. Obviously, they and you want the bank to approve your mortgage should you be seeking a home loan.

Your mortgage payment should be close to or under your current rent payments. If your current rent is difficult for you, be sure your monthly mortgage payment is less.

There should be a mortgage calculator at most real estate websites. Not everyone needs a 30 year mortgage. Use it to see what your mortgage payments would be for a 30 year, 20 year, 15 year or 10 year loan.

You want to pay off your loan as soon as possible. Own your home free and clear as soon as you possibly can. That's real freedom!

Set up Bi-Weekly Payments to Pay off Mortgage Faster:

Upon approval, see if your bank will allow you to divide your mortgage to be paid every two weeks (i.e. 50% on the 1st and 50% on the 15th). This allows you to pay off your mortgage faster. If possible, have this automatically deducted from your bank account on scheduled payments just as you did with your first time home buyer's club program.

You want to be able to make payments comfortably and on time so your home does not go into foreclosure. Your rent is a good indicator as to what your mortgage will likely be. However, your ideal payment should be less than your current monthly rent.

The bank will review all your paperwork more in depth once you have selected the property you wish to purchase. They will review your credit score, income, value of property as collateral and your ability to pay. Therefore, it is important that you take this time to prepare your paperwork and get your credit up to par for smooth sailing.

Work Sheet

Step 9 – Home Search

Once you've been pre-approved for a mortgage, you can begin your home search. Although your home is your castle, be sure to shop for properties within the amount for which you or you and your spouse have been approved and can comfortably afford.

Today, most realtors will ask you if you've been pre-approved before they start showing you homes. Most will recommend you get pre-approved for a home loan unless you are paying cash and even then, some will ask for proof of funds. No one wants to run around wasting time on people who just want to look at homes, but do not qualify to buy.

Real Estate Websites:

You may want to start your search online. If you have access to a computer, begin by looking at local real estate websites. You can also search general websites which include all properties listed in the MLS such as Zillow.com or Trulia.com to name a few.

Upgrade or Turnkey:

Enter the minimum number of bedrooms and bathrooms you or your family needs as well as the price range. (*minimum 3 bedroom/ 2 bath or larger have best resale value*). Just because you've been pre-approved for a certain amount doesn't mean you have to pay your maximum price. You may find some good deals if you are willing to do some upgrades. Remember, many of these programs have free money for home improvements.

Some people just prefer to move into a turn-key property which means all the work is done. You just have to get the keys and move in. Those people are usually willing to pay full price for the added convenience. That's okay too. It's a personal choice.

Location. Location. Location.

Location is very important. Find a neighborhood that suits you. Younger people may be willing to move into up and coming areas. Time is on their side. Others prefer to live within a certain radius of their workplace. Some people need access to public transportation. Keep all these factors in mind when selecting homes you want your realtor to show you. There is no need to look at homes that don't fit your major criteria.

Stay away from homes next to major highways and dump sites. A good location will allow your property to increase in value. This helps when you are ready to sell.

Find a Realtor:

Once you've selected a few homes you'd like to see, contact a realtor. *(See Realtors.com)* A good realtor can help you in your search by sending new property listings that fit your criteria when they first hit the market.

It helps to know what you want. Don't make the realtor guess or decide for you. Once you are clear on what you need, the realtor can send you daily property listings by email or text as they arise.

If that realtor is not responsive to your needs, choose another. However, do not continue seeing properties with the other realtor if you've found someone who is more sensitive to your needs. Let them know you are working with someone else.

City Renovated Properties:

Your city should also have a website link for properties they have already renovated and are now making available to first time home buyers. There are not usually as many but the renovation work has already been done. They are usually located in areas the city is trying to develop.

Additional free grants are often associated with these properties for those who qualify. The programs often pay all or part of the down payment and closing costs for first time home buyers.

However, they want people who are committed to the upkeep of these properties. Therefore, they often require a longer commitment of living in the home than other grants (i.e. 15 years or so). Speak to the housing counselor about the requirements. This is very convenient for people who see themselves living in the community long term.

Work Sheet

What are your property search criteria? How many bedrooms and bathrooms do you need? List properties you are considering. Visit open houses.

Work Sheet

Work Sheet

Step 10 - Purchase Offer

Purchase Offer:

Once you've selected a home that fits your family needs, it's time to submit an offer. Tell your realtor, this is the one.

Ask your realtor for the comps in the area. Comps are recent property sales of similar properties in the area. That should help you make a reasonable offer.

You will then go back to the realtor's office to submit an offer to the seller. If you are buying a city renovated property, you will likely submit an offer through your Home Buyer Counselor at the city office building. It's good to have your realtor at the meeting or your real estate attorney on speed dial. Ask your realtor if you have any questions.

Attach Earnest Money/Down Payment:

Depending on the property and your bank requirements, this can be anywhere from 5-20% of the asking price. However in some instances, including properties that meet the city's first time home buyer's club, this can be as little as $1,000. Just ask. They will hold the down payment in escrow until you close on the property.

Real Estate Attorney:

You will need a **real estate attorney** when submitting an offer. If you don't already have one, ask your realtor for a referral. They are also listed in the yellow pages in the phone book or do a search online. Do not get any other type of attorney. They specialize in real estate and usually have one flat fee.

Your Purchase Offer states the amount you are willing to pay for the property. The seller is usually given 24-48 hours to approve or reject the offer.

Contingency Clause:

Be sure to put in your contingency clause, "**subject to attorney approval**". If anything goes wrong during the pre-purchase process, you can always call your attorney and tell him or her to cancel the deal and get your deposit back.

You may also include subject to **inspector approval** and/or **bank lender (*a.k.a. mortgage*) approval** later when the offer is approved. The real estate attorney approval clause is a must. It can cover all of the above.

Step 11 – Get Property Inspected

Once your offer is approved, you've set a "soft" closing date. It's just an estimate as you may or may not need the seller to make some changes for the deal to close and you will have to wait until the free money grant checks are all ready and lined up at the attorney's office to help pay for the closing costs.

Fully Insured - State Certified - Home Inspector

Now it's time to get the property inspected. Contact a fully insured, state certified home inspector. You can also go to ASHI.org. *Do not use an associate in training*. Some of the free money grants may also cover home inspection. Get a receipt. Feel free to check with the Better Business Bureau if you need further validation.

The bank and city will each also have their own house inspection before approving your funding. After all, the property is what is being held as collateral until you've completed paying for your new home. However, it is wise that you get your own inspection done too.

 If the house needs a new roof or any damage in the foundation or some other item that could be costly for you, then you can go back to the seller and ask them to fix it, lower the asking price, or provide credit at closing for you to make the necessary remedies yourself. The home inspector's fee is worth the small investment for your long term peace of mind. You need to know what you're getting into. It's either a wise investment for you and your family or a money pit you want to avoid. In that event, you can select another house that works for you.

Some people don't mind a "fixer upper". But know the costs in advance. Bring in a licensed contractor to the house to give you a cost estimate before making a final decision.

Be sure to factor in the cost of the house, any repairs or upgrades, and the time it will take to complete. Ask what grants if any are available should you decide to do so.

Remember, if there are major repairs, you may have to continue paying rent while your new home is getting upgrades. Unless you are staying with family or friends, or living on the property while under construction, you may be paying rent and a mortgage.

Plan in advance. Decide what works best for you.

Work Sheet

Did the property pass inspection? If not, what needs to be done? Will you pay for major repairs or the seller? Are there any grants that cover the upgrades/repairs needed?

Work Sheet

Step 12 – Grant & Mortgage Approval

Contact Housing Counselor:

Once your offer is approved, your realtor will submit your paperwork to the city to start the free money grant process. They will inspect the property you've chosen and start preparing the checks for which you've qualified.

Final Bank Approval:

Contact your bank where you've received pre-approval mortgage and let them know you've selected a property. Your realtor will usually do this for you. The realtor will submit the documents to your bank and your real estate attorney.

Your bank will then schedule an inspection of the property and let you know if you've been approved. This is the final approval you will need based on your current credit, income, and the value of the property which is the collateral for the loan. The home must be worth at least the value of the loan money requested or more.

If the property is worth more, that's even better. The difference in value will be the home equity you have available. It's always good to enter a home that already has some equity whenever possible. Short sales offer this opportunity, but the process can sometimes be lengthy waiting for approval.

Once the city and your bank have inspected the property and approved you for the grant money (covers down payment/closing costs/ sometimes repairs) and the home loan, you are near closing on your new home.

Work Sheet

Work Sheet

Step 13 - Title Documents

Stay on Top of Every Step!

Once your bank has approved your mortgage, your realtor will send the paperwork to your attorney for title inspection. However, you must stay on top of every step.

We've provided this workbook and the checklist (see page 83) herein for you to make sure every step is completed and your realtor is on top of everything. Because some realtors are not getting their usual 6% commission but rather a flat broker's fee for some of these first time home buyers programs, they may or may not be as motivated. However, you should be 100% interested in the status of your first home.

Be polite, but persistent. No one cares about your new home more than you.

Remember, these people are working for you. Just because you are not buying a multi-million dollar property (yet), you should still be getting proper service. These people are still getting paid. You may be doing business together again when you're ready to sell.

Your attorney is also receiving a standard flat fee. Real estate attorneys do this all the time. They know the process. Unless there is something that needs remedy, they should be able to complete their part rather quickly.

Your attorney will usually contact you within a couple of days if there is some matter that needs your attention. Otherwise, the completed paperwork (title documents – history of the property) should be intact at closing.

Never be afraid to pick up the phone and contact your realtor or real estate attorney if things are taking a bit long. This is not unusual. Remember, you need all your elements in place to be ready at closing.

Work Sheet

Work Sheet

Step 14 – Get Home Insurance

Before you close on the property, your mortgage lender will require you to obtain home owner's insurance. Check around for the best rates.

You may already have renter's insurance or car insurance. If so, then speak to your broker about bundling. You can often get better rates when you get your home and car insurance from the same broker.

You may or may not have to have already paid your homeowner's insurance in advance. However, if you have started the policy, your broker may simple send you a statement or invoice marked PAID to show that you have opened an account and have arranged payment.

Regardless, forward it to your realtor before closing. Your mortgage lender will need it before signing off on your home loan.

Work Sheet

Do you already have car, life, or renter's insurance? Can you bundle your package with your current broker or some other with better rates?

Work Sheet

Step 15 – Closing

Free Money Grants from City:

Your realtor will call you when the city and bank have each completed their home inspections and have processed your paperwork. The city's home buying counselor will let your realtor know when the checks are ready. All parties can then confirm a mutually agreeable day and time for closing.

You will receive your check from the city to cover any agreed grants at closing. This will either supplement your down payment/closing costs or go towards the principle, or home repairs.

First Time Home Buyers Club Funds:

Your bank will add the matching funds to your first time money club account balance. This can often be up to four times what you deposited.

This should cover your down payment, closing costs, and any workshop fees you may have had to attend. Some banks or cities also include grants that will reimburse you for additional expenses. Know what they are in advance so as not to delay the process.

Assume nothing. Ask anything. Get receipts.

Transfer Bank Lender (Mortgage) Funds:

Your bank will then transfer funds from the approved mortgage lender to the seller's account. Contracts will be signed. Receive the keys to your new home!

Step 16 – Move In!

Congratulations!

It's time to move into your first home. Some grants may require you move in to your new home within two weeks of closing on the house. However, some of you will have some minor or major repairs or upgrades before the final move in date. Work this out in advance before confirming your first mortgage payment date with your lender. You want to start your new chapter on the right foot. That means making payments on time.

If you are getting work done on the house, you will either still be paying rent or staying with friends or family while the work gets done. If you still have an apartment lease, speak to your real estate attorney about how to get out of it due to your home purchase.

Planning in advance, patience, and maintaining open lines of communication with all parties concerned paves the road for your success. Celebrate your achievement!

Work Sheet

New Locks & Keys:

The first thing you need to do when you move in is to get new locks on the doors, and replace any automatic garage door openers. So many people have been coming in and out of the property including the previous home owners. You don't want any surprises. The new locks will let everyone know with keys to the property, there's a new home owner. That's you!

The seller is usually required to leave the home in move in condition. However some of the properties have been sitting on the market for a while including some short sales. You and some family and friends may want to come in and clean the house from top to bottom before moving in. You can also hire a cleaning service to do this if you have budgeted accordingly.

Step 18 – Post Purchase Workshop

Most of these first time home buyer grants will require a follow up workshop. This is standard with any grant. They want to make sure you are complying with the agreement.

It's usually a brief workshop just to review how everything is coming along. They want to make sure you are not in over your head. It's a good time to voice any concerns or any unexpected surprises about home ownership.

They want you to be a happy and successful home owner. It also helps them to know if they are preparing people properly. Home budgeting and maintenance is usually discussed. You can also confer with other new home owners.

Just be clear about your commitment. The grants are to increase the number of potential homeowners who may not have afforded it in the past. They expect these people to help them build the communities. That means keeping your home clean inside and out, building relationships, and deferring crime in the community.

This helps children and families to feel safe in their communities. The home investment helps to build the local and national economy too. It also helps strengthen the housing market which in turn increases job opportunities.

You see? There is a domino effect. Everyone involved benefits.

Work Sheet

Work Sheet

Important Closing Remarks

Be sure you know the minimum amount of time you are expected to live in your new home. Many of the grants have a second position lien on the property after the mortgage lender. This is no problem. Most people take as long to save the money for down payment and closing costs as the time period of the second lien. However, take note.

After the grant period has expired, just have the lien from the grant provider removed. This is often the same bank or credit union where you started your first time home buyer's club and have your mortgage. Others are funded through the city.

Keep all this information together in a safe place for easy access. You will need to know this in the event you decide to sell your home after the grant period has expired.

Work Sheet

What is your grant term period? Keep this information in a safe place along with your mortgage and grant agreements to have the data removed when the grant term expires.

Work Sheet

Keep a Check List

Checklist

Get Free Copy of Credit Report _____

Join First Time Home Buyers Club – FTHBC (Bank/Credit Union) _____

Schedule auto-deposits with payroll for FTHBC Acct _____

Build Your Credit (3 Revolving Credit Accts) _____

(i.e. Major Credit Card, Dept. Store, Gas Card, Car Payments)

Ask if employer offers "matching funds" for first home buyers _____

Complete Home Buyer's Assistance Program Application _____

(*Contact Local City Gov't Real Estate – Home Division*)

Set Interview with Home Buyer's Assistance Counselor _____

Complete Interview with Home Buyer Counselor _____

Attend Homeowners Workshop _____

Get Pre-Approved for Home Loan _____

Begin Home Search _____

Find a Real Estate Attorney _____

Select Home _____

Make Offer (Submit Purchase Offer) _____

Get Offer Approved _____

Receive Mortgage Commitment _____

Real Estate Attorney Completes Title Documents _____

Submit Paperwork for City for Property Inspection _____

Complete Your Own Home Inspection _____

Get Attorney Approval _____

Get Homeowner's Insurance _____

Close on Property _____

Move in to your NEW Home! _____

Attend Post-Purchase Class _____

Notes

Notes

"Through wisdom is a house built; and by understanding is established: And by knowledge shall the chambers be filled with precious and pleasant riches."

~ Proverbs 24:3-4

Get Additional Workbooks and DVDs:

Get additional **Free Money to Buy Your Fir$t Home** workbooks and DVDs and find other inspirational material on our website **www.SoRichIam.com**

Groups:

Want to start your own workshop at your church, with friends, family or social group? We provide discounts for bulk purchases via www.lulu.com/SoRichIam *(case sensitive)*

Pay it forward!

Many people don't believe they can be home owners. Now you know they can! Please share this workbook and DVD with others. Go to Amazon.com and click on the share (email) or Twitter or Facebook link. Thank you in advance!

If you enjoyed this reading, you may also appreciate **The Answer Key to Avoid Debt, Build Credit & Retire Rich** *(A Guide to Lifetime Prosperity for Students, Grads, DropOuts & DropIns)*! Find it at www.SoRichIam.com and on Amazon.

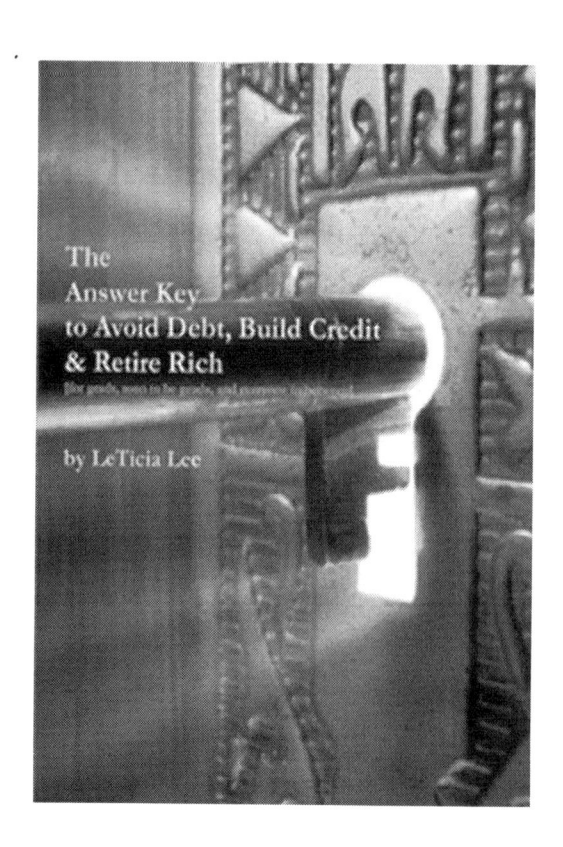

When you purchased this book, you not only helped yourself, but many others too. A portion of every purchase goes to churches and charities worldwide that help feed, clothe, and shelter people in underserved communities. Thank you!

"A good man leaves an inheritance to his children's children; and the wealth of the sinner is laid up for the just."

Proverbs 13:22

Made in the USA
Charleston, SC
16 September 2014